NINTENDO 64®
SECRET CODES
3

IIIIIIBRADYGAMES
TAKE YOUR GAME FURTHER™

NINTENDO 64® SECRET CODES 3

LEGAL STUFF

Brady Publishing

An Imprint of
Macmillan Digital Publishing USA
201 West 103rd Street
Indianapolis, Indiana 46290

ISBN: 1-56686-892-0

Library of Congress Catalog No.: 99-072443

Printing Code: The rightmost double-digit number
is the year of the book's printing; the rightmost
single-digit number is the number of the book's
printing. For example, 99-1 shows that the first
printing of the book occurred in 1999.

01 00 99   3 2 1

Manufactured in the United States of America.

BRADYGAMES STAFF

Publisher
Lynn Zingraf

Editor-In-Chief
H. Leigh Davis

Title/Licensing Manager
David Waybright

Marketing Manager
Janet Eshenour

Acquisitions Editor
Debra McBride

Creative Director
Scott Watanabe

Assistant Licensing Manager
Ken Schmidt

Assistant Marketing Manager
Tricia Reynolds

CREDITS

Development Editor
David Cassady

Project Editor
Tim Cox

Screenshot Editor
Michael Owen

Book Designers
Tanja Pohl
Brian Tolle

Production Designer
Dan Caparo

TABLE OF CONTENTS

NINTENDO 64® SECRET CODES 3

Control Pad —

Control Stick —

C-Left Button

C-Up Button

B Button

A Button

C-Right Button

C-Down Button

ALL-STAR BASEBALL '99

Play as the Alien Abductors
Enter **ATEMYBUIK** at the Cheat menu. Then at the Stadium Select screen, choose Alienapolis Park.

Big Ball
Enter **BBNSTRDS** at the Cheat menu.

Fat or Skinny Players
Enter **ABBTNCSTLO** at the Cheat menu.

Ball Trail Mode
Enter **GRTBLSFDST** at the Cheat menu.

• •

A
B
C
D
E
F
G
H
I
J
K
L
M
N
O
P
Q
R
S
T
U
V
W
X
Y
Z

ALL-STAR BASEBALL 2000

Big Ball
Enter **BCHBLKTPTY** at
the Enter Cheats menu.

Blurry
Enter **MYEYES** at the
Enter Cheats menu.

Lights Out Mode
Enter **WTOTL** at the
Enter Cheats menu.

● ●

BANJO-KAZOOIE

Bottles Bonus Codes
After getting the puzzle
piece inside the castle
in Treasure Trove Cove,
return to Banjo's Home.
Face the picture of
Bottles on the wall and

WAHAY! YOU'VE FOUND MY
SECRET 'MOVING PICTURE'

press C-Up to look closer. This should take you to a puzzle.

Piece together the puzzle within the time limit to access a code. You will then get a chance at another puzzle. After each puzzle, you will get the codes listed below. Bottles will tell you there are no more puzzles after

HA...FOOLED YOU! I'VE GOT ONE REALLY SPECIAL

the sixth one, but look at the picture again to get the seventh and final puzzle.

After solving this puzzle, return to the picture to get a recap of the codes you have learned. Enter these codes at the castle in Treasure Trove Cove to access the desired effect.

You can enter **NOBONUS** to cancel the code.

Puzzle	Code	Effect
1st	BOTTLESBONUSONE	Big head
2nd	BOTTLESBONUSTWO	Big arms and legs
3rd	BOTTLESBONUSTHREE	Small head and tall body
4th	BOTTLESBONUSFOUR	Kazooie has big head and wings
5th	BOTTLESBONUSFIVE	Big heads and feet
6th	BIGBOTTLESBONUS	A combination of the above
7th	WISHYWASHYBANJO	Turns Banjo into Washer (Kazooie's invisible)

200 Eggs

After breaking the rock on the path to the left of the Freezezy Peak puzzle, return to Bubble Gloop Swamp and turn into the Alligator. Go through the opening created by breaking the rock to find the Spell Book.

Now you can enter the code **BLUEEGGS** at the castle in Treasure Trove Cove to receive 200 eggs and a limit of 200 eggs.

100 Red Feathers

While at Mad Monster Mansion turn into the pumpkin, exit the world, and head up the path to find Brentilda. Enter the small hole near Brentilda, and follow the path until you find a Spell Book.

Now enter the code **REDFEATHERS** at the castle in Treasure Trove Cove to receive 100 red feathers and a limit of 100 feathers.

20 Gold Feathers

There are three pipes to the right of the Rusty Bucket Bay entrance. Enter the middle pipe and throw the switch to raise the water. While in the water, go to the right. You should find another Spell Book.

Now enter the code **GOLDFEATHERS** at the castle in Treasure Trove Cove to receive 20 gold feathers and a limit of 20 feathers.

Refill All Items
After finding all three Spell Books, enter **BLUEREDGOLDFEATHERS** at the castle in Treasure Trove Cove.

Infinite Gold Feathers
Enter **CHEAT** at the castle in Treasure Trove Cove, and then enter **AGOLDENGLOWTOPROTECTBANJO**.

Infinite Lives
Enter **CHEAT** at the castle in Treasure Trove Cove, and then enter **LOTSOFGOESWITHMANYBANJOS**.

Infinite Air
Enter **CHEAT** at the castle in Treasure Trove Cove, and then enter **GIVETHEBEARLOTSOFAIR**.

Maximum Energy
Enter **CHEAT** at the castle in Treasure Trove Cove, and then enter **ANENERGYBARTOGETYOUFAR**.

Infinite Eggs
Enter **CHEAT** at the castle in Treasure Trove Cove, and then enter **BANJOBEGSFORPLENTYOFEGGS**.

Infinite Mumbo Tokens
Enter **CHEAT** at the castle in Treasure Trove Cove, and then enter **DONTBEADUMBOGOSEEMUMBO**.

Infinite Red Feathers
Enter **CHEAT** at the castle in Treasure Trove Cove, and then enter **NOWYOUCANFLYHIGHINTHESKY**.

••••••••••••••••••••••••••••••••••••

BATTLETANX

Trippy Mode
Enter **CNCTHRTM** at the Input Code screen.

Run Story
Enter **CDPLT** at the Input Code screen.

Unlimited Ammo
Enter **LTSFBLLTS** at the Input Code screen.

Unlimited Lives
Enter **LVFRVR** at the Input Code screen.

Invulnerable
Enter **MSTSRVV** at the Input Code screen.

Invisible
Enter **CRSTLCLR** at the Input Code screen.

Frogs
Enter **FRGZ** at the Input Code screen.

Toads
Enter **TDZ** at the Input Code screen.

Hurl Mode
Enter **HVRL** at the Input Code screen.

Choose Gang in Campaign Mode
Enter **LTSLTSGNGS** at the Input Code screen. After starting a Campaign, you should be able to select a gang.

Storm Ravens Gang
Enter **WMNRSMRTR** at the Input Code screen.

Passwords

Level	Password
1	FRHBWNTNTK
2	LHTTTBKRLS
3	RCJRWPCLGM
4	VVSLGGVHRF
5	LPFFLNHJJF
6	CTMGPRWGBH
7	HPJMKGMCJV
8	WHSNKNFRGS
9	CRFPHGCTKP
10	HHRBKPVWGB
11	WFHMKCFWLB
12	SPLJTFLRFS
13	LTSLTSGNGS

BODY HARVEST

All Weapons

Enter your name as **ICHEAT** and start a new game.
During gameplay, press A, Right, C-Down, C-Right,
C-Up, A, Left.

Fat Legs

Enter your name as **ICHEAT** and start a new game. During gameplay, press Left, A, Right, Down.

More Powerful Weapons

Enter your name as **ICHEAT** and start a new game. During gameplay, press C-Down, C-Up, Up, Z, Z, Left, C-Right.

Mutant Alien

Enter your name as **ICHEAT** and start a new game. During gameplay, press C-Down, Up, Z, Z, C-Right, Right.

Surreal Mode

Enter your name as **ICHEAT** and start a new game. During gameplay, press C-Down, Up, Right, Right, C-Right, A, Left.

Smart Bomb

Enter your name as **ICHEAT** and start a new game. During gameplay, press A, C-Up, C-Up, Up + Left.

Very Easy Difficulty

At the Difficulty Select screen, press Left repeatedly until it says "Very Easy."

Very Hard Difficulty

At the Difficulty Select screen, press Right repeatedly until it says "Very Hard."

• •

BUCK BUMBLE

All Weapons

At the Title screen, press Left, Right, Up, Down, then hold Z and press Right, Right, Left, Left. Start a game and press A + B + R Shift to refill life and ammo.

Level Select

At the Title screen, hold Z and press Right, Down, Down, Right. Then release Z and press Right, Up, Down, Left, Left, Up, Right, Right.

Infinite Lives

At the Title screen, press L Shift, R Shift, B, A, Z, Left, Right.

CALIFORNIA SPEED

Fog Color

Select a single race or practice. Immediately hold L Shift + R Shift + C-Up + C-Down + C-Left + C-Right +

Down until the Track Select screen appears. You should find a new option to adjust fog color.

• •

CHARLIE BLAST'S TERRITORY

Passwords

DESERT ISLANDS

Level	Password
2	4 Clubs, 5 Hearts, 10 Clubs, Queen Clubs, Queen Clubs
3	4 Clubs, 5 Hearts, 10 Spades, 9 Clubs, 4 Clubs
4	Ace Clubs, 7 Diamonds, 6 Hearts, 6 Spades, 2 Hearts

Level	Password
5	6 Hearts, 2 Hearts, Ace Spades, 5 Hearts, 8 Hearts
6	9 Diamonds, 10 Diamonds, Jack Diamonds, Jack Hearts, Queen Hearts
7	9 Diamonds, 10 Hearts, 10 Hearts, 7 Diamonds, 5 Hearts
8	Ace Clubs, 7 Diamonds, 8 Diamonds, 5 Clubs, 8 Hearts
9	6 Diamonds, 4 Hearts, 9 Hearts, 6 Hearts, Queen Clubs
10	7 Diamonds, 10 Hearts, Ace Hearts, 9 Spades, 6 Hearts

ALPINE ISLANDS

Level	Password
11	7 Diamonds, 4 Spades, 9 Diamonds, 7 Hearts, Queen Hearts
12	6 Diamonds, 4 Diamonds, 9 Clubs, 8 Clubs, 4 Clubs
13	5 Spades, 9 Spades, Jack Hearts, 6 Clubs, 4 Clubs
14	2 Hearts, 3 Diamonds, 9 Diamonds, 3 Diamonds, 2 Clubs
15	4 Clubs, 5 Hearts, Queen Spades, 4 Clubs, 8 Clubs
16	6 Diamonds, Jack Spades, 2 Hearts, Ace Diamonds, 6 Hearts
17	6 Hearts, 2 Hearts, Queen Clubs, 7 Spades, 3 Hearts

Level	Password
18	6 Clubs, King Hearts, 10 Hearts, Ace Clubs, 3 Spades
19	2 Hearts, 3 Diamonds, 7 Hearts, 6 Clubs, 10 Diamonds
20	6 Diamonds, Jack Clubs, 3 Hearts, 4 Clubs, 8 Hearts

TROPICAL ISLANDS

Level	Password
21	Ace Clubs, Jack Spades, 3 Clubs, 7 Hearts, 9 Hearts
22	9 Hearts, 6 Clubs, 2 Hearts, 6 Spades, 2 Spades
23	2 Hearts, 3 Diamonds, 7 Clubs, Queen Hearts, 8 Diamonds
24	Ace Clubs, 7 Diamonds, 6 Spades, Jack Clubs, 4 Hearts
25	Ace Clubs, Jack Clubs, 3 Diamonds, Jack Hearts, King Hearts
26	4 Clubs, 6 Hearts, 8 Clubs, Queen Spades, Ace Diamonds

● ●

A
B
C
D
E
F
G
H
I
J
K
L
M
N
O
P
Q
R
S
T
U
V
W
X
Y
Z

CHOPPER ATTACK

Debug Menu

At the Press Start screen, press and hold Z and press Right, Left, Up, Down, A, B, Start.

EXTREME-G 2

To access the following modes of play, enter the following codes as your name. You can turn off the following codes by entering the code again.

Press R Shift at the Vehicle Selection screen to access the Name Entry screen.

Blurry Mode

Enter your name as
FLICK.

Overhead View
Enter your name as **SPYEYE**.

Rotating Camera
Enter your name as **SPIRAL**.

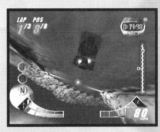

Tron Mode
Enter your name as **NEUTRON**.

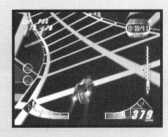

No Fog/Pop Up
Enter your name as **PIXIE**.

Unlimited Nitro
Enter your name as **NITROID**.

Unlimited Shields and Lasers
Enter your name as **XCHARGE**.

Unlimited Weapons
Enter your name as **MISTAKE**.

Wireframe Mode
Enter your name as
LINEAR.

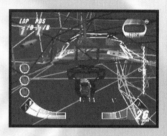

Plane Mode
Enter your name as
2064.

No Screen Panels
Enter your name as **NOPANEL**.

Level Skip
Enter your name as **RA50**. While racing, pause the
game and quit. You can now advance to the next
race.

Random Course in Time Trials
Enter your name as **JUGGLE**.

Remove an Engine
Enter your name as **MISPLACE**.

To access the following EXTREME-G 2 codes,
enter the following codes at the Password
screen.

Venom Superbike
Enter the password
868QCMH3H9HT.

Wasp Superbike
Enter the password
55Hz1MH3H9H1.

Super Speed
Enter the password
XXX.

. . . .

F-ZERO X

All Machines, All Courses, and Master Difficulty

At the Mode Select screen, press L Shift, Z, R Shift, C-Up, C-Down, C-Left, C-Right, Start.

Smaller Machines

At the Machine Select screen, press and hold L Shift + R Shift, and then press C-Left + C-Down.

• •

FIFA ROAD TO WORLD CUP '98

Creations Software Team
At the Stadium Select screen, press R Shift to access the Team Management options. Select Customize Player and change the player's name to **BuryFC**.

....

FORSAKEN 64

Level Select
At the Title screen, press A, R Shift, Z, Up, Up, C-Up, C-Down, C-Down.

Invincibility
At the Title screen, press A, Z, Z, Up, Left, C-Left, C-Left, C-Down.

Stop Enemies Cold
At the Press Start screen, press R Shift, Z, Right, Right, C-Up, C-Left, C-Right, C-Down.

Infinite Primary Weapon
At the Press Start screen, press A, R Shift, Z, Right, C-Up, C-Right, C-Down, C-Down.

Infinite Secondary Weapon
At the Press Start screen, press B, B, Z, Left, Left, C-Up, C-Left, C-Right.

A
B
C
D
E
F
G
H
I
J
K
L
M
N
O
P
Q
R
S
T
U
V
W
X
Y
Z

Infinite Weapon Energy

At the Press Start screen, press L Shift, Z, Left, Right, Down, Down, C-Down, C-Down.

One-Shot Kills

At the Press Start screen, press B, B, B, L Shift, R Shift, Left, Down, Down.

••

FOX SPORTS COLLEGE HOOPS '99

30 Second Quarter

Enter **THIRTY** at the Secret Code menu.

Alternate Commentary

Enter **MONKEY** at the Secret Code menu.

Big Heads

Enter **NOGGIN** at the Secret Code menu.

Disable Shot Clock

Enter **BUZZZ** at the Secret Code menu.

No Crowd
Enter **NOFANS** at the
Secret Code menu.

Play as the Design Team
Enter **TEAM-Z** at the
Secret Code menu.

Play on Z-Axis Court
Enter **Z-WOOD** at the Secret Code menu.

Trails Follow Ball
Enter **TRAILS** at the Secret Code menu.

Transparent Players
Enter **GHOST** at the
Secret Code menu.

GLOVER

Fish Eye
Pause the game and press C-Left, C-Right, C-Left, C-Right, C-Left, C-Right, C-Left, C-Right.

Open Portals
Pause the game and press C-Up, C-Right, C-Right, C-Down, C-Left, C-Down, C-Up, C-Right.

Play as Frog
Pause the game and press C-Up, C-Right, C-Down, C-Right, C-Up, C-Left, C-Left, C-Up. Now each time you eat a bug, you gain a life.

Infinite Life
Pause the game and press C-Up (X5), C-Right, C-Down, C-Right.

Speed-up Spell
Pause the game and press C-Left, C-Left, C-Right, C-Up, C-Right, C-Left, C-Down, C-Down.

Secret Cheat

Pause the game and press C-Down, C-Up, C-Right, C-Right, C-Down, C-Left, C-Right, C-Right.

Call Ball

Pause the game and press C-Up, C-Left, C-Left, C-Up, C-Right, C-Left, C-Down, C-Up.

Control Ball

Pause the game and press C-Left, C-Right, C-Left, C-Right, C-Up, C-Down, C-Right, C-Right.

Checkpoints

Pause the game and press C-Down, C-Down, C-Right, C-Left, C-Up, C-Up, C-Down, C-Left.

Death Spell

Pause the game and press C-Up, C-Left, C-Left, C-Left, C-Left, C-Up, C-Right, C-Up.

Low Gravity

Pause the game and press C-Left, C-Left, C-Up, C-Left, C-Right, C-Up, C-Up, C-Up.

A
B
C
D
E
F
G
H
I
J
K
L
M
N
O
P
Q
R
S
T
U
V
W
X
Y
Z

Shift Camera Left

Pause the game and press C-Right, C-Down, C-Right, C-Down, C-Up, C-Up, C-Right, C-Left.

Shift Camera Right

Pause the game and press C-Left, C-Right, C-Up, C-Up, C-Down, C-Right, C-Down, C-Right.

Power Ball

Pause the game and press C-Up, C-Down, C-Up, C-Down, C-Up, C-Down, C-Left, C-Up.

Big Glover (Hercules)

Pause the game and press C-Down, C-Down, C-Down, C-Left, C-Left, C-Down, C-Right, C-Left.

Frog Spell

Pause the game and press C-Down, C-Left, C-Down, C-Down, C-Left, C-Down, C-Up, C-Left.

Locate Garibs
Pause the game and press C-Left, C-Up, C-Right, C-Down, C-Left, C-Up, C-Left, C-Left.

Infinite Energy
Pause the game and press C-Right, C-Right, C-Down, C-Right, C-Right, C-Right, C-Up, C-Left.

Level Select
Pause the game and press C-Up, C-Up, C-Up, C-Left, C-Left, C-Right, C-Left, C-Right. Now quit your game and then at the Main Menu press Up, then A to access the Level Select menu.

Enemy Ball
Pause the game and press C-Left, C-Down, C-Up, C-Right, C-Left, C-Left, C-Down, C-Down.

Turn Off Cheats
Pause the game and press C-Down (X8).

••••••••••••••••••••••••••••••••••••

IGGY'S RECKIN' BALLS

Hidden Characters
At the Player Select screen, press Z, A, Left, Right.

All Tracks
At the Title screen,
press R Shift + Z to
access the Cheat screen.
Enter **THEUNIVERSE** as
the cheat.

All Hidden Players (Except Iggy's Girlfriend)
At the Title screen,
press R Shift + Z to
access the Cheat screen.
Enter **HAPPYHEADS** as
the cheat.

Tiny Characters
At the Title screen, press R Shift + Z to access the
Cheat screen. Enter **MICROBALLS** as the cheat.

Different Surfaces

At the Title screen, press R Shift + Z to access the Cheat screen. Then enter the following codes for:

Platform	Password
Icy Platforms	*ICEPRINCESS*
Gooey Platforms	*GOOEYGOOGOO*

••••••••••••••••••••••••••••••••••

INTERNATIONAL SUPERSTAR SOCCER 64

Six Hidden All-Star Teams

Defeat the league mode or press Up, L Shift, Up, L Shift, Down, L Shift, Down, L Shift, Left, R Shift, Right, R Shift, Left, R Shift, Right, R Shift, B, A, and then hold down Z and press Start at the Title screen. When entered correctly, you will hear "What an incredible comeback!"

Big Head Mode

Press C-Up, C-Up, C-Down, C-Down, C-Left, C-Right, C-Left, C-Right, B, A, and then hold down Z and press Start at the Title screen. When entered correctly, you will hear "Goal!"

••••••••••••••••••••••••••••••••••

KEN GRIFFEY JR.'S SLUGFEST

Automatic Home Run

When batting as Ken Griffey, press Left, Left, Right, Right, Right, Left, Left on the D-Pad before the pitch. Now just make contact with the pitch to hit a home run.

KOBE BRYANT IN NBA COURTSIDE

Alien Heads for Left Field

Press C-Up, C-Down, C-Left, C-Right, Start, Start, A, B, A, R Shift, and Z at the Main menu. Select the Left Field Team to give them Alien Heads.

Big Head Mode

During gameplay, press Right, Right, Left, R Shift, Z, Start, A, Start, A, Start, Z. (You must enter this code using Controller 1.)

Big Head Mode (Without Starting a Game)
When you see the picture of Kobe Bryant after turning on the game, quickly press Right, Right, Left, R Shift, Z, Start, A, Start, A, Start, Z.

•••••••••••••••••••••••••••••••••••••••

KNIFE EDGE: NOSE GUNNER

Tougher Difficulty
As the Kemco logo appears on-screen, hold R Shift + L Shift + C-Up, and then press C-Right, C-Left, and B.

Stage Select
Go to the Story or Team mode and enter the following while the stage number is being displayed: Press and hold all four C-Buttons and R Shift, and then press Right, Up, Left, and Down.

•••••••••••••••••••••••••••••••••••••••

LODE RUNNER 3-D

Level Select
Pause the game, hold Z and press R Shift, B, A, B, A, C-Up, C-Down, C-Left, C-Right, C-Up, C-Down, C-Left, C-Right. A new option called **Unlock Worlds** should appear.

•••••••••••••••••••••••••••••••••••••••

MADDEN NFL '99

Bonus Stadiums

At the Code Entry screen, enter **OUR-HOUSE** to play at the Tiburon Stadium.

Bonus Teams

Enter the following at the Code Entry screen:

Code	Team
BESTNFC	NFC Pro Bowl
AFCBEST	AFC Pro Bowl
BOOM	All-Madden Team
IMTHEMAN	All-Time Stat Leaders
PEACELOVE	60s Greats
BELLBOTTOMS	70s Greats

SPRBWLSHUFL	80s Greats
HEREANDNOW	90s Greats
TURKEYLEG	All-Time Greats
THROWBACK	75th Anniversary Team

Code	Team
GEARGUYS	*NFL Equipment Team*
WELCOMEBACK	*1999 Cleveland Browns*

INTHEGAME	*EA Sports*
HAMMERHEAD	*Tiburon*

Tomato Quarterback
Enter **SPLAT** at the Code Entry screen.

Turbo Mode
Enter **TURBO TIME** at the Code Entry screen.

••••••••••••••••••••••••••••••••••••••

A B C D E F G H I J K L M N O P Q R S T U V W X Y Z

MAJOR LEAGUE BASEBALL FEATURING KEN GRIFFEY

Dancing Pitcher
While pitching, press Up, Up, Down, Left, Left, Right, Right, Left, Left, Down, Up, Up.

Dancing Batter
While batting, press Up, Up, Down, Left, Left, Right, Right, Left, Left, Down, Up, Up.

• •

MARIO PARTY

Bumper Ball Maze 1
Reach the goal of Mini-Game Island and defeat Toad in a game of Slot Car Derby 2. Bumper Ball Maze 1 will now be available in the Mini-Game House.

Bumper Ball Maze 2
Clear all 50 Mini-Games on Mini-Game Island and talk to Toad at the Goal. Bumper Ball Maze 2 will now be available in the Mini-Game House.

Bumper Ball Maze 3

After setting new records on Bumper Ball Mazes 1 and 2 (under 1 minute), Bumper Ball Maze 3 will become available.

Easy Money

In the Option House, go to Mini-Game Stadium. Set the computers on hard, use handicaps and set 50 coins for each player, and set it for 30 turns. When you near the end of the game, turn the computer players to human players so that you can get all of the coins they have collected.

Eternal Star Board

Complete each board in Standard Mode (35 Turns), earn 100 stars, and visit the Bank.

Magma Mountain Board

Complete each board in Standard Mode (35 Turns). Magma Mountain should now be available at the Mushroom Shop for 980 coins.

A B C D E F G H I J K L M N O P Q R S T U V W X Y Z

No Boo and No Koopa

After defeating Mario Party by earning 100 stars and finishing the Eternal Star board, No Boo and No Koopa become available in the Mushroom Shop.

• •

MICRO MACHINES 64 TURBO

Cheat Codes

Pause the game and enter the following. You will hear a beep when entered correctly. To disable a code, just reenter it.

Effect	Code
Any Object	*Down, Down, Up, Up, Right, Right, Left, Left*
Big Bounces	*C-Left, Right, Right, Down, Up, Down, Left, Down, Down*
Double Speed	*C-Left, C-Down, C-Right, C-Left, C-Up, C-Down, C-Down, C-Down, C-Down*
Slow CPU Cars	*C-Right, C-Up, C-Left, C-Down, C-Right, C-Up, C-Left, C-Down*

Debug Mode

Pause the game and press C-Left, Up, Down, Down, C-Left, C-Right, C-Right, C-Up, C-Down. This enables you to access the following during gameplay:

Effect	Code
Win Race	Press Z + C-Down (doesn't work in time trials)
Rotate Camera	Hold Z and press Up, Down, Left or Right
Zoom Camera	Hold Z and press L Shift or R Shift
Change Into Drone	Hold Z and press C-Left
Blow Up All Cars	Press C-Down + C-Up + C-Right + C-Left.

● ●

MIKE PIAZZA'S STRIKE ZONE

Hidden Message

Before the Title screen appears, press C-Up, R Shift, B, B.

Change Skies

At the Team Select screen, press L Shift, R Shift, L Shift, R Shift, and then press C-Right, A, Z, C-Up, L Shift, R Shift, Z.

Aluminum Bats

At the Team Select
screen, press L Shift,
R Shift, L Shift, R Shift,
then press R Shift, A, Z,
B, A, L Shift, L Shift.

Red Bats

At the Team Select screen, press L Shift, R Shift,
L Shift, R Shift, then press R Shift, Down, B, A,
Right.

Blue Bats

At the Team Select screen, press L Shift, R Shift,
L Shift, R Shift, then press B, L Shift, B, A.

Colorful Bats

At the Team Select
screen, press L Shift,
R Shift, L Shift,
R Shift, then press
Z, B, R Shift, A.

Crazy Ball

At the Team Select screen, press L Shift, R Shift, L Shift, R Shift, then press C-Right, A, Z, B, A, L Shift, L Shift.

Crazy Pitch

At the Team Select screen, press L Shift, R Shift, L Shift, R Shift, then press C-Right, A, Z, C-Up, R Shift, B.

Devil's Thumb Stadium

At the Team Select screen, press L Shift, R Shift, L Shift, R Shift, then press Right, A, C-Up, L Shift, A.

Easy Steals

At the Team Select screen, press L Shift, R Shift, L Shift, R Shift, then press C-Left, A, Down, C-Up, Z.

Faster Gameplay

At the Team Select screen, press L Shift, R Shift, L Shift, R Shift, then press L Shift, A, Z, R Shift, B, A, L Shift, L Shift.

High Gravity

At the Team Select screen, press L Shift, R Shift, L Shift, R Shift, then press Up, Down, L Shift, Up, R Shift.

Low Gravity

At the Team Select screen, press L Shift, R Shift, L Shift, R Shift, then press Up, R Shift, A, L Shift.

Slower Gameplay

At the Team Select screen, press L Shift, R Shift, L Shift, R Shift, then press Up, L Shift, L Shift, B, A, L Shift, L Shift.

Varied Pitches

At the Team Select screen, press L Shift, R Shift, L Shift, R Shift, then press C-Right, A, Z, C-Up, R Shift, L Shift.

All Hits Are Homeruns

At the Team Select screen, press L Shift, R Shift, L Shift, R Shift, then press L Shift, A, C-Down, C-Right.

All Players Ratings to 10

At the Team Select screen, press L Shift, R Shift, L Shift, R Shift, then press B, A, R Shift, B, A, L Shift, L Shift.

•••

MILO'S ASTRO LANES

Enter the following codes while the ball is rolling down the lane. You are only allowed one code per turn and three codes per match.

Clone Ball

Press L Shift, L Shift, L Shift, R Shift, R Shift, R Shift.

White Dwarf

Press R Shift, R Shift, R Shift, L Shift, L Shift, L Shift.

Turbo Ball

Press R Shift, R Shift, L Shift, L Shift, R Shift, L Shift.

Mega Ball

Press L Shift, L Shift, R Shift, R Shift, L Shift, R Shift.

•••

MISSION: IMPOSSIBLE

Big Feet Mode

At the Level Select screen, press C-Down, R Shift, Z, C-Right, C-Left. When entered correctly, you will hear Ethan say "That's better."

Big Head Mode

At the Level Select screen, press C-Down, R Shift, C-Up, L Shift, C-Left. When entered correctly, you will hear Ethan say "That's better."

Giant Head Mode

At the Level Select screen, press C-Down, L Shift, C-Up, C-Right, L Shift. When entered correctly, you will hear Ethan say "That's better."

Kid Mode

At the Level Select screen, press C-Down, C-Up, R Shift, L Shift, Z. When entered correctly, you will hear Ethan say "That's better."

Turbo Mode

At the Level Select screen, press C-Up, Z, C-Up, Z, C-Up. When entered correctly, you will hear Ethan say "That's better."

Mini Rocket Launcher

At the Level Select screen, press R Shift, L Shift, C-Left, C-Right, C-Down. When entered correctly, you will hear Ethan say "That's better."

7.65 Silenced Handgun

At the Level Select screen, press C-Up, L Shift, C-Right, C-Left, C-Up. When entered correctly, you will hear Ethan say "That's better."

9mm Handgun

At the Level Select screen, press R Shift, L Shift, C-Down, C-Up, C-Up. When entered correctly, you will hear Ethan say "That's better."

Uzi

At the Level Select screen, press C-Right, C-Left, C-Right, C-Down, R Shift. When entered correctly, you will hear Ethan say "That's better."

• •

NASCAR '99

Finish in the top five at the following tracks in a Championship Season with at least 50 percent race length to access the following hidden drivers:

Driver	Track
Bobby Allison	*Charlotte*
Davey Allison	*Talladega*
Alan Kulwicki	*Bristol*
Benny Parsons	*Richmond*
Cale Yarborough	*Darlington*
Richard Petty	*Martinsville*

Hidden Drivers

Select Single Race from the main menu and choose the following tracks. Then highlight Select Car and enter the corresponding code.

Driver	Track	Code
Bobby Allison	*Charlotte*	*C-Up, C-Left, C-Down, C-Right, L Shift, R Shift, L Shift, R Shift, Z, Z*

Driver	Track	Code
Davey Allison	*Talladega*	*C-Up, C-Left, C-Down, C-Right, L Shift, R Shift, L Shift, R Shift, L Shift, R Shift*

Alan Kulwicki   Bristol   Z (X8), R Shift, R Shift

Benny Parsons   Richmond   C-Up, C-Right, C-Down, C-Left, Z, Z, Z, L Shift, Z, Z

Richard Petty   Martinsville   C-Up, C-Up, C-Down, C-Down, C-Left, C-Right, C-Left, C-Right, L Shift, R Shift

. . . .

A B C D E F G H I J K L M N O P Q R S T U U W X Y Z

NBA JAM '99

Giant Players

Pause the game and press L Shift, L Shift, C-Right, L Shift, L Shift, C-Right, L Shift, L Shift, C-Right, Z.

Tiny Players

Pause the game and press L Shift, L Shift, C-Left, L Shift, L Shift, C-Left, L Shift, L Shift, C-Left, Z.

Make Your Next Shot

Pause the game and press L Shift, L Shift, C-Up, L Shift, L Shift, C-Up, L Shift, L Shift, C-Up, Z.

Dunk from Anywhere

Pause the game and press L Shift, L Shift, C-Down, L Shift, L Shift, C-Down, L Shift, L Shift, C-Down, Z.

Super Push

Pause the game and press L Shift, L Shift, Up, L Shift, L Shift, Up, L Shift, L Shift, Up, Z.

Tie the Score

Pause the game and press L Shift, L Shift, Down, L Shift, L Shift, Down, L Shift, L Shift, Down, Z.

Team On Fire

Pause the game and press L Shift, L Shift, Right, L Shift, L Shift, Right, L Shift, L Shift, Right, Z.

Cancel Cheats

Pause the game and press L Shift, L Shift, Left, L Shift, L Shift, Left, L Shift, L Shift, Left, Z.

••••••••••••••••••••••••••••••••

NFL BLITZ

During the **Today's Match-up** screen, use the Turbo, Jump, and Pass buttons to enter the following codes. To enter the code, press **Turbo** to enter the first number of the code, **Jump** for the second number, **Pass** for the third number, and then press the D-pad in the noted position.

For example, for the "No CPU Assistance" code, don't press Turbo, press Jump one time, press Pass two times, and press the D-pad Down. A message appears on-screen to confirm the code.

No CPU Assistance
0 1 2 Down

Computer offers no help during gameplay

Tournament Mode
1 1 1 Down

Turns off codes and CPU assistance

Smart CPU Opponent
3 1 4 Down

CPU more skilled

Show Field Goal %
0 0 1 Down

Shows field goal percentage after each field goal

No Play Selection
1 1 5 Left

Selects a random play; in two-player mode, both players must enter code

Night Game
2 2 2 Right

Play game at night

Turn Off Stadium
5 0 0 Left

Gets rid of stadium

Show More Field
0 2 1 Right

Shows entire width of
field; in two-player
mode, both players
must enter code.

No First Downs
2 1 0 Up

Player must score in four downs

No Punting
1 5 1 Up

Disables punts; in one-player mode, CPU can still
punt.

No Random Fumbles
4 2 3 Down

No random fumbles, although you can still fumble if you get hit while jumping or spinning.

No Interceptions
3 4 4 Up

Can't throw interceptions; note that both players must enter code.

Late Hits
0 1 0 Up

Enables even later hits than normal

Hide Receiver Name
1 0 2 Right

Covers up receiver's names

Stepping Out
2 1 1 Left

Enables stepping out of bounds (as opposed to jumping out)

Weather: Rain
5 5 5 Right

Weather: Clear
2 1 2 Left

Weather: Snow
5 2 5 Down

Big Head
2 0 0 Right

Player's head twice its normal size

Huge Head
0 4 0 Up

Player's head four
times its normal size

Team Big Head
2 0 3 Right

Big heads for whole
team

Headless Team
1 2 3 Right

Whole team is headless

No Head
3 2 1 Left

The player you control has no head

Invisible
4 3 3 Up

Player with ball is invisible

Team Big Players
1 4 1 Right

Increases size of players

Team Tiny Players
3 1 0 Right

Decreases size of players

Big Football
0 5 0 Right

Increases size of ball

Super Field Goals
1 2 3 Left

Enables longer kicks, although you still need to be accurate

Super Blitzing
0 4 5 Up

Faster blitzes

Hyper Blitz
5 5 5 Up

Infinite Turbo, No First Downs, Super Field Goals (both players must enter code)

Infinite Turbo
5 1 4 Up

Turbo never runs out

Fast Turbo Running
0 3 2 Left

Turbo makes player move even faster

A
B
C
D
E
F
G
H
I
J
K
L
M
N
O
P
Q
R
S
T
U
V
W
X
Y
Z

Power-up Teammates
2 3 3 Up

Stronger team

Fast Pass
2 5 0 Left

Bullet passes

Power-up Blockers
3 1 2 Left

More powerful offensive line

Power-up Speed
4 0 4 Left

Faster players (both players must enter code)

Power-up Defense
4 2 1 Up

Stronger defense

Power-up Offense
3 2 1 Up

Stronger offense

Secret Characters

To play as the following secret characters, enter the name and PIN number of the player of your choice at the **Record Keeping** screen. The announcer will make a comment if entered correctly.

Name:	**PIN:**	
TURMEL	0322	
SAL	0201	
JASON	3141	
JENIFR	3333	
DANIEL	0604	
JAPPLE	6660	

A
B
C
D
E
F
G
H
I
J
K
L
M
N
O
P
Q
R
S
T
U
V
W
X
Y
Z

ROOT	6000	
LUIS	3333	
MIKE	3333	
GENTIL	1111	
FORDEN	1111	
VAN	1234	
CARLTN	1111	

THUG	1111	
SKULL	1111	
BRAIN	1111	
SHINOK	8337	
RAIDEN	3691	

....

NFL QUARTERBACK CLUB '99

Enter the following at the Cheat menu:

Code	Effect
SCLLYMLDR	Alien stadium
PWRPYLNS	Huge pylons
BGMNY	Big coin in the coin toss
MRSHMLLW	Big players

Code	Effect
BCHBLL	Super size football
TRBMN	Unlimited turbo
STCKYBLL	No fumbles
FRRSTGMP	Play in slow motion
DBLDWNS	8 downs
XTRTMS	Hidden teams
XTRVLTG	Electric football mode
BTTRFNGRS	Always fumble
HSNFR	Smoking ball
PNBLL	Players bounce around like pinballs
FLBBR	Flubber ball
PPCRNRTRNS	Land mines
PWRKCKR	Super kickers

Code	Effect
RGBY	*Rugby mode*
HSPTL	*Mega-injuries*

Code	Effect
TTHPCK	*Skinny players*
RCQTBLL	*Racquetball mode*
SLPNSLD	*Slippery mode*

●●●●●●●●●●●●●●●●●●●●●●●●●●●●●●●●●●●

NHL '99

Enter the following codes at the Password
screen:

Code	Effect
BIGBIG	*Big players*
BRAINY	*Big heads*
FAST	*Faster gameplay*
FASTER	*Even faster gameplay*
FLASH	*Flashing cameras*
FREEEA	*Unlocks EA Blades and EA Storm*
PULLED	*No goalies*

●●●●●●●●●●●●●●●●●●●●●●●●●●●●●●●●●●●

NHL BREAKAWAY '99

Cheat Menu

At the Main menu, press C-Left, C-Right, C-Left, C-Right, R Shift, R Shift.

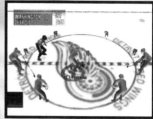

Extra Bonus Points

At the Season menu, press C-Left, C-Left, C-Right, C-Right, C-Left, C-Left, C-Right, C-Right, R Shift, R Shift to add 100 bonus points.

•••••••••••••••••••••••••••••••••••••

NIGHTMARE CREATURES

Cheat Menu

Press C-Down, Up, Left, Down, Down, C-Left, C-Left, C-Right as a password. This will give you an option for unlimited lives and items, the option to play as a monster, and a level select.

Passwords

Level	Password
2	Up, Down, C-Up, C-Down, C-Up, Down, Left, C-Right
4	Up, Left, C-Up, C-Down, C-Up, Left, C-Up, C-Right
5	Up, C-Down, C-Up, Left, C-Up, C-Left, C-Down, Left
9	Up, Right, C-Up, C-Down, C-Up, C-Up, C-Right, C-Right
11	Down, Left, C-Up, Down, C-Up, C-Right, C-Left, Up
13	Down, C-Left, Right, C-Down, Up, C-Down, Down, Up
14	Down, C-Down, C-Right, C-Left, C-Up, C-Up, Left, C-Up
16	Left, C-Left, C-Up, C-Left, C-Up, Down, C-Right, C-Left

OFF-ROAD CHALLENGE

El Cajon Track

At the Track Select screen, hold Up and press L Shift + R Shift. You should hear an air wrench. Highlight El Paso, hold Z, and press the gas.

Flagstaff Track

At the Track Select screen, hold Left and press L Shift. You should hear an air wrench. Highlight Mojave, hold Z, and press the gas.

Guadalupe Track

At the Track Select screen, hold Down and press R Shift. You should hear an air wrench. Highlight Vegas, hold Z, and press the gas.

Extra Trucks

There are eight trucks in the game. Press each C-Button to access a new truck.

RAMPAGE 2: UNIVERSAL TOUR

Play as George
Enter the password **SM14N**.

Play as Lizzie
Enter the password **S4VRS**.

Play as Ralph
Enter the password
LVPVS.

Play as Myukus
Enter the password **NOT3T**.

Play as Alternate to Myukus
Enter the password
B1G4L.

RUSH 2: EXTREME RACING USA

Bonus Cars

Hidden keys activate the bonus cars in Rush 2. With every fourth key that you collect, you will activate another car from the following:

Taxi, Hot Rod, Formula 1, Prototype, Mountain Dew Racer

You need all 12 keys to unlock the Prototype. Collect all four Mountain Dew cans to unlock the Mountain Dew Racer.

Cheat Menu

To access the Cheat menu, hold L Shift + R Shift + Z at the Setup screen. While still holding those buttons, press all four C-Buttons. When done correctly, the Cheats option should appear under Audio.

To access the codes in the Cheat menu, place the cursor on the code you want to access and then enter one of the following:

Note: Where the abbreviation (x#) is indicated, you may need to press the combination the number of times indicated in the code. Also, you can randomly press Z + L Shift + R Shift + all the C-Buttons to get the codes (with the exception of Stunts).

Effect	Code
Mass	*Hold L Shift + R Shift, and press C-Up, C-Down, C-Left, C-Right*
Killer Rats	*Hold L Shift + R Shift, and press Z, Z, Z, Z*
New York Cabs	*Press R Shift, L Shift, Z, C-Up, C-Down, C-Up*

Resurrect in Place	*Hold Z + C-Left and press C-Right, then hold Z + C-Right and press C-Left*

Frame Scale	*Hold Z + C-Down and press C-Up, then hold Z + C-Up and press C-Down*

Effect	Code
Tire Scaling	Hold Z + C-Left and press C-Right, then hold Z + C-Right and press C-Left

Effect	Code
Auto-Abort	Press C-Up (X4)
Burning Wreck	Hold C-Up and press Z (X4)
Gravity	Hold Z and press C-Left, C-Up, C-Right, C-Down (X3)
Car Collisions	Hold L Shift + R Shift, and press C-Left, C-Up, C-Right, C-Down (X3), then press Z
Cone Mines	Hold Z and press L Shift and R Shift (X4)
Car Mines	Press Z + C-Up, then C-Right, C-Down, C-Left (X6)
Track Orientation	Hold L Shift + R Shift, and press C-Up, C-Right, C-Down, C-Left (X4)
Super Speed	Hold L Shift + R Shift, and press C-Up, C-Down, C-Left, C-Right
Inside-Out Car	Hold C-Right + C-Down, and press L Shift, R Shift, Z, L Shift, R Shift, Z

Effect	Code
Damage	*Press R Shift, C-Down, L Shift (X2)*
Invincible	*Press L Shift, C-Up, R Shift (X2)*
Invisible Car	*Hold L Shift + R Shift, and press C-Up, C-Down (X5)*

Invisible Track	*Hold L Shift + R Shift, and press C-Down, C-Up (X5)*

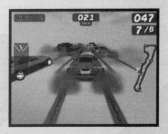

Effect	Code
Brakes	Hold C-Up + C-Right, and press Z (X3)
Super Tires	Hold L Shift + R Shift, and press C-Up, C-Right, C-Down, C-Left (X2)
Suicide Mode	Hold Z, and press C-Down, C-Left, C-Up, C-Right (X2)
Do the Dew!	Press L Shift + R Shift + C-Down, then L Shift + R Shift + C-Left, then L Shift + R Shift + C-Up, then L Shift + R Shift + C-Right (X2), then Z.
Levitation	Hold L Shift + R Shift + Z, and press C-Up (X4)
Fog Color	Hold Z and press C-Left + C-Up + C-Right + C-Down (X3)
Game Timer	Hold Z + C-Down and press C-Up, then hold Z + C-Up and press C-Down
Stunts	Hold all 4 C-Buttons, press R Shift, A, Z, L Shift

S.C.A.R.S

Cobra Car
Enter the password **TRTTLL**.

Scorpion Car
Enter the password **SDSSRT**.

....

SNOWBOARD KIDS 2

All Characters, Boards, and Courses
At the Title screen, press Z, B, C-Up, and Down
(on the Control Pad), Left (on the Control Stick),
Right (on the Control Stick), Up (on the Control
Pad), R Shift, Z, A.

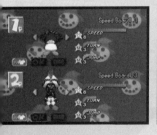

....

SOUTH PARK

Master Cheat
Enter the password **BOBBYBIRD**.

All Characters in Multiplayer Mode
Enter the password **OMGTKKYB**.

All Weapons
Enter the password **FATKNACKER**.

Big Head Mode
Enter the password **MEGANOGGIN**.

Level Select
Enter the password **THEEARTHMOVED**.

Pen and Ink Mode

Enter the password **PLANEARIUM**.

Unlimited Ammo

Enter the password **FATTERKNACKER**.

Bonus Characters

To access a character in Multiplayer Mode, enter one of the following passwords:

Password	Character
VEGGIEHEAVEN	Skinny
CHEATINGISBAD	Mr. Mackey
ELVISLIVES	Bar Brady
OUTRAGE	Big Gay Al
HAWKING	Ned
SLAPUPMEAL	Starvin Marvin
PHAERT	Phillip
RAFT	Terrance
DOROTHYSFRIEND	Mr. Garrison
LOVEMACHINE	Chef
CHECKATACO	Wendy
FISHNCHIPS	Pip
KICKME	Ike
ALLWOMAN	Mrs. Cartman
GOODSCIENCE	Mephisto
STARINGFROG	Jimbo
MAJESTIC	Alien

A B C D E F G H I J K L M N O P Q R S T U V W X Y Z

SPACE STATION: SILICON VALLEY

Bonus Game

At the Zone Select screen, press Down, Up, Z, L Shift, Down, Left, Z, and Down. You should hear a sound when entered correctly. Enter a zone and return to the Zone Select screen.

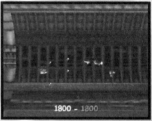

STAR WARS EPISODE 1: RACER

Cheat Codes

Select an empty file and then press and hold Z. To enter the following codes, press L Shift at each letter, highlight End, and then press L Shift:

Code	What It Does
RRJINNRE	*Unlock Mars Guo, enter this code, and then name the file A. Select the game with Mars Guo available to access a new driver, Jinn Reeso, in place of Phuii.*

RRDUAL	*This code enables a dual controller setup, where each controller controls a separate engine. Player 1 uses a controller plugged into port 1 and one in port 3. Player two uses ports 2 and 4.*
RRJABBA	*This code makes you almost invincible. During gameplay, pause the game and press Left, Down, Right, Up to access the Cheat menu.*
RRTHEBEAST	*This code gives you Mirror Mode. During a game you must pause the game and press Left, Down, Right, Up on the D-Pad to access the cheat menu.*

STAR WARS: ROGUE SQUADRON

Credits
Enter **CREDITS** at the Passcode screen.

Radar
Enter **RADAR** at the Passcode screen for a different radar.

AT-ST Bonus Level
Enter **CHICKEN** at the Passcode screen.

All Power-Ups
Enter **TOUGHGUY** at the Passcode screen.

Fly the Millennium Falcon

Enter **FARMBOY** at the Passcode screen.

Fly the Tie Interceptor

Enter **TIEDUP** at the Passcode screen. At the Ship Select screen, highlight the Millennium Falcon and press Up to access the Tie Interceptor.

Level Select

Enter **DEADDACK** at the Passcode screen.

Increase Difficulty

Enter **ACE** at the Passcode screen.

Infinite Lives

Enter **IGIVEUP** at the Passcode screen.

Fly a Cadillac

Enter **KOELSCH** at the Passcode screen. The V-Wing will now be a Cadillac.

Music Menu and Ship Gallery

Enter **MAESTRO** at the Passcode screen.

Watch All Cut-Scenes

Enter **DIRECTOR** at the Passcode screen.

Alternate Title Screen

Enter **HARDROCK** at the Passcode screen. Return to the Title screen and Luke's face will be replaced with another.

SUPER SMASH BROS.

Earn Captain Falcon

Play as one character all the way through the 1-Player challenge within 15 minutes. After the game's credits, you'll get challenged to a one-on-one duel with

Captain Falcon. If you can defeat him, he'll appear in in the upper-right of the player lineup.

Earn Jigglypuff

Play as one character all the way through the 1-player challenge after earning Captain Falcon. After the credits, JigglyPuff will challenge you. If you win the fight, she'll appear in the lower-right of the the character roster

A
B
C
D
E
F
G
H
I
J
K
L
M
N
O
P
Q
R
S
T
U
V
W
X
Y
Z

Earn Luigi

To get Luigi in your roster, you must defeat the Bonus Stage 1 levels for each of the eight original characters, either in Practice or the 1-Player mode. Then Luigi will challenge you to a fight.

After defeating him, he'll appear in you're the upper-left of the character roster.

Earn Ness

Start a 1-Player game, set the difficulty to "Normal," and the set the amount of lives to three. Choose a character and take him/her through the game without continuing. If you

accomplish this challenge, Ness will appear after the credits and challenge you. Defeat him and he'll appear in the lower-left position of the roster.

Earn Mushroom Kingdom

First, defeat the game with the original eight characters on Normal difficulty with three stock. Then enter each Multiplayer stage once.

Earn Sound Test

After earning every character in the game, head into Bonus Stage 1 and Bonus Stage 2 and complete each task with all the characters. You'll then be informed that you've earned the Sound Test. Now access the main Options menu to listen to every song, speech, and sound in the game.

Earn Item Switch

Play 100 rounds of
Multiplayer to earn the
Item Switch menu. Now
access the Options menu
to choose how often
power-ups will appear in
Multiplayer mode. You
can turn on and off the
frequency of each item
in the game.

TOP GEAR OVERDRIVE

Open Up Cars and Seasons

There are four options at the Main menu:
Championship, Versus, Setup, and Credits. Think
of them numerically, starting from 0 to 3. (For
example, Championship is 0, Versus is 1, and
so on.)

You can input the following codes by highlighting
the appropriate menu item and pressing Z. You
should hear an engine rev when entered correctly.

Effect	Code
Open Normal Cars	3, 0, 0, 1
Open Hot Dog Car	3, 1, 2, 0, 1, 1
Open Nintendo Power Car	0, 3, 1, 2, 1, 0, 2, 3
Open Taco Car	1, 1, 0, 3, 0, 1, 0, 3, 2, 1, 2
Open All Cars	3, 3, 1, 3, 2, 0, 0, 0, 1
Start with Season 4	1, 0, 0, 3, 2, 2, 0
Start with Season 5	2, 0, 3, 1, 1, 2, 0, 1, 3, 0
Start with Season 6	3, 2, 1, 0, 0, 3, 0, 1, 2, 0, 3, 2, 2
View ending credits	2, 2, 0, 1

TRIPLE PLAY 2000

Add a Run for Away Team
During gameplay, hold L Shift + R Shift + Z and press
C-Right, C-Right.

Add a Run for Home Team
During gameplay, hold
L Shift + R Shift + Z and
press C-Left, C-Left.

3 Balls
While batting, hold L Shift + R Shift + Z and press
Up, Down.

3 Outs
During gameplay, hold L Shift + R Shift + Z and press
Down, Up.

Easy Strike Out
During gameplay, hold L Shift + R Shift + Z and press
Up, Right, Up, Right.

Easy Home Run

During gameplay, hold L Shift + R Shift + Z and press Left, Up, Left, Up. Simply make contact with the ball to hit a home run.

● ●

TUROK 2: SEEDS OF EVIL

Big Cheat

Enter **BEWAREOBLIV-IONISATHAND** at the Enter Cheat screen, and then turn on this option at the Cheat Menu screen.

Big Hands and Feet Mode

Enter **STOMPEM** at the Enter Cheat screen, and turn it on at the Cheat Menu screen.

Big Head Mode

Enter **UBERNOODLE** at the Enter Cheat screen, and turn it on at the Cheat Menu screen.

Blackout Mode

Enter **LIGHTSOUT** at the Enter Cheat screen, and turn it on at the Cheat Menu screen.

Gouraud Mode

Enter **WHATSATEXTUREMAP** at the Enter Cheat screen, and turn it on at the Cheat Menu screen.

Pen-and-Ink Mode

Enter **IGOTABFA** at the Enter Cheat screen, and turn it on at the Cheat Menu screen.

Stick Men Mode

Enter **HOLASTICKBOY** at the Enter Cheat screen, and turn it on at the Cheat Menu screen.

Tiny Enemy Code

Enter **PIPSQUEAK** at the Enter Cheat screen, and turn it on at the Cheat Menu screen.

Fruit Stripes
Enter **FROOTSTRIPE** at the Enter Cheat screen, and turn it on at the Cheat Menu screen.

Zach Mode
Enter **AAHGOO** at the Enter Cheat screen, and turn it on at the Cheat Menu screen.

Juan's Cheat
Enter **HEEERESJUAN** at the Enter Cheat screen, and turn it on at the Cheat Menu screen.

View Credits
Enter **ONLYTHEBEST** at the Enter Cheat screen, and turn it on at the Cheat Menu screen.

• •

VIGILANTE 8

Alien Vehicle
Enter the password **GIMME_DA_ALIEN**.

All Levels and Characters

Enter the password
JTBT7CFD1LRMGW.

All Vehicles Except the Alien

Enter the password
GANGS_UNLOCKED.

Bonus Level

Complete "Y" the Alien's quest.

Choose the Same Car in Multiplayer

Enter the password
MIX_MATCH_CARS.

Ultra-High Resolution

Enter the password
MAX_RESOLUTION.

Enhanced Missiles

Enter the password **MISSILE_ATTACK**.

God Mode

Enter the password **LIVING_FOREVER**.

Rapid-Fire

Enter the password **FIRE_NO_LIMITS**.

Reduced Gravity

Enter the password
A_MOON_GETAWAY.

Remove All Enemies
Enter the password **POPULATION_OUT**.

Slow Motion
Enter the password **GO_REALLY_SLOW**.

Super Hard Difficulty
Enter the password **I_AM_TOUGH_GUY**.

Unlock Levels
Enter the password
LEVEL_SHORTCUT.

View All Endings
Enter the password
LONG_SLIDESHOW.

Secret Moves

Weapon	Secret Move	Move	Cost
Interceptor Missiles	Halo Decoy	Up, Up, Down, Fire Machine Gun	2 Missiles
Bull's Eye Rockets	Stampede	Up, Down, Up, Fire Machine Gun	5 Rockets
Sky Hammer Mortar	Turtle Turnover	Down, Down, Down, Fire Machine Gun	2 Shells
Bruiser Cannon	Cow Puncher	Down, Up, Down, Fire Machine Gun	2 Shells
Roadkill Mines	Cactus Patch	Left, Right, Up, Fire Machine Gun	2 to 6 Mines

• •

V-RALLY EDITION '99

Bonus Cars

At the Press Start screen, press L Shift + R Shift, C-Left, C-Right, L Shift + R Shift. Then at the Options screen, hold Z and press L Shift.

A B C D E F G H I J K L M N O P Q R S T U V W X Y Z

Cheat Menu

At the Press Start screen, press L Shift + R Shift, C-Left, C-Right, L Shift + R Shift, and then press Start. At the next screen, hold Z and press L Shift until the Cheat Mode appears.

. . . .

WCW NITRO 64

All Wrestlers

At the Title screen, press C-Right (X4), C-Left (X4), R Shift (X4), L Shift (X4), and Z.

Extra Rings

At the Title screen, press C-Left, L Shift, C-Right, R Shift, C-Left, L Shift, C-Right, R Shift, and Z.

Head Swells When Wrestler Gets Hit

At the Title screen, press C-Left (X7), L Shift, and Z.

Big Heads

At the Title screen, press C-Right (X7), R Shift, and Z.

Do the YMCA

Select the Disco ring, then during gameplay press B.

Big Heads, Hands and Feet

At the Title screen, press R Shift (X7), C-Right, and Z.

Ring Select

At the Options menu, highlight the ring option and press C-Right, R Shift, C-Right, R Shift, Z. When entered correctly, you should hear a sound. Enter this again to access the next ring. To return to a previous ring, press C-Left, L Shift, C-Left, L Shift, and Z.

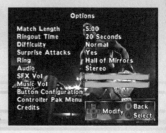

Hidden Characters— One at a Time

Highlight a Wrestler and press C-Left, C-Right, L Shift, R Shift, C-Left, C-Right, L Shift, R-Shift, Z.

. . . .

WCW/NWO REVENGE

Play as THQ Man

Highlight AKI Man and press C-Down.

Play as Curt Hennig
Win the U.S. Heavyweight.

Play as Rowdy Roddy Piper
Win the World Heavyweight Belt.

Play as Kidman
Win the Cruiserweight Belt.

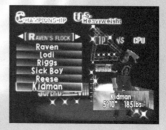

Play as Meng and Barbarian
Win the Tag Team Belts.

Play as Kanyon
Win the TV Title.

Play as Mortis
After accessing Kanyon, highlight Kanyon and press any C-Button.

Play as Managers
During a One-on-One Exhibition Match, choose a wrestler who has a manager. During gameplay, press Z on the third and fourth controllers.

Steal Opponents Special Move
When your character's Spirit Meter is flashing, grapple your opponent and press A + B.

A
B
C
D
E
F
G
H
I
J
K
L
M
N
O
P
Q
R
S
T
U
V
W
X
Y
Z

WIPEOUT 64

Infinite Energy

During gameplay, hold Z + L Shift + R Shift and press C-Up, C-Down, C-Left, C-Right, C-Up, C-Down, C-Left, C-Right.

Infinite Weapons

During gameplay, hold Z + L Shift + R Shift and press C-Down, C-Down, C-Left, C-Left, C-Right, C-Right, C-Up.

Piranha II

Complete the Time Challenge mode with Bronze or better.

Velocitar Track

Complete Race mode with a Bronze or better.

Cyclone Weapons

Complete the Weapons Challenge mode with a Bronze or better.

Super-Combo Challenge

Complete the three challenge modes

All Teams

At the Main menu,
hold Z + L Shift +
R Shift and then press
C-Down (X4), C-Right,
C-Up, C-Left. The
screen will flash
green when entered
correctly.

....

WWF WARZONE

Earning Cheats

You earn cheats by winning the Challenge mode
with different characters. To access the Cheat
menu, press L Shift, then R Shift at the Main
menu.

Trainer

Enter the Training mode. The trainer will be
available as a Custom Wrestler.

Cactus and Dude

Defeat the Challenge mode on Medium or Hard difficulty with Mankind.

Extra Outfits—Stone Cold

Defeat the Challenge mode on Medium difficulty with Steve Austin. This gives you extra outfits for Steve Austin.

Extra Outfits—Goldust

Defeat the Challenge mode on Medium difficulty with Goldust. This gives you extra outfits for Goldust.

Ladies Night

Defeat the Challenge mode on Medium difficulty with Shawn Michaels or Triple H. This enables you to select a female in the Create A Wrestler option.

Sue, the Ring Girl

Defeat the Challenge mode on Medium or Hard difficulty with Bret Hart or Owen Hart. Now Sue, the Ring Girl, will be selectable as a Custom Wrestler.

Additional Outfits

Defeat the Challenge mode on Medium difficulty with Kane. This creates more outfit options in the Create A Wrestler option.

Modes

You can turn on or off the following options by accessing the Cheat menu after earning the option. All the modes must be turned off to earn points for Custom Wrestlers.

Big Head

Defeat the Challenge mode on Medium difficulty with The Rock or British Bulldog.

Polished

Defeat the Challenge mode on Medium difficulty with any character.

No Meters

Defeat the Challenge mode on Medium difficulty with the Undertaker.

A B C D E F G H I J K L M N O P Q R S T U V W X Y Z

Ego Mode

Defeat the Challenge mode on Medium difficulty with Ahmed Johnson.

Beans Mode

Defeat the Challenge mode on Medium difficulty with Thrasher or Mosh.

No Blocking

Defeat the Challenge mode on Medium difficulty with Faarooq or Ken Shamrock.